This Book Belongs To:

How To Benefit From This Activity Book:

This book is intended to help you explore your inner beliefs about common life events that cause many people emotional and mental disturbance.

The questions and activities in this book were created by Jannet Harper, a licensed clinical therapist in Florida.

The questions and activities are loosely based on the Cognitive Behavioral Therapy intervention. Each question prompts you to explore how you really feel, not just your immediate reactions in different situations.

Some Cognitive Behavioral Therapy Basics:

This intervention is used during talk therapy to guide you into understanding where your core beliefs lie and how that impacts your behavior (or reaction) in situations.

A- is the situation (Activating Event) - Put Your Own situation in the blank. The ityped information is just an example.

B- is the belief (this is the thought/belief that immediately kicks in. Often, without you realizing the thought/belief is involved in the situation.)

C- consequence of B - or your usual/immediate reaction to A. This is what we want to change by dealing with unhealthy beliefs in B.

What to do next

If the activities in this book lead you to want to go into a deeper conversation about your situations, beliefts and actions then please learn more about resources below:

Our Therapy Services:
Www.HolisticCoaching.info/healingtherapy
~Individuals & Couples~
Www.HolisticCoaching.info/bookaservice

Learn More About Our Business Services if the activities in this book lead you to want to go into a deeper conversation about your hurdles to accomplishment, goals, and strategy.

Www.HolisticBizMarketing.com/professional-therapy
~Individuals & Couples in Business~
Www.HolisticBizMarketing.com/booknow

Additional Nationwide (US) Resources:

Suicide Prevention Hotline: 1.800.273.8255 (TALK) or dial 988
Sexual Assault Hotline: 1.800.656.4673
Addiction Help: 1.800.662.4357

Housing Resources:
https://affordablehousingonline.com/open-section-8-waiting-lists

Belief vs Behavior

Activating Event: "Falling for someone new"
Put the Activating Event in your own words:

____

Belief: What do you expect out of a relationship?
Example: How would you describe what you want
during a relationship?)
Put your Beliefs in Descriptive Terms:

____

____

____

____

Consequences (Actions): How do you behave when
you do not get what you expect out of a
relationship? Example: When you're emotionally hurt
do you want to lash out in anger, keep it in or vent?
Put your Actions in Descriptive Terms:

____

____

____

____

Word Chase ~ How Many Words Can You Make?

_e_l_ng   C__s_t

B_n_s   H_pp_ness

_k_l_t_n   C_ut__g

Mood Tracker

J F M A M J J A S O N D

1
2
3
4
5
6
7
8
9
10
11
12
13
14
15
16
17
18
19
20
21
22
23
24
25
26
27
28
29
30
31

AMAZING

HAPPY

NORMAL

EXCITED

STRESSED

FOCUSED

TIRED / EXHAUSTED

DEPRESSED / SAD

SICK

LOW ENERGY

NERVOUS/ ANXIOUS

ANGRY

Assign color to a specific mood
and color the squares according to
your mood

Belief vs Behavior

Activating Event: "Recognizing Undesirable Character Traits"

Put the Activating Event in your own words:

____

Belief: How do you feel about these traits/behaviors?
Example: Every time he shuts down during a dicussion it makes me angry because I feel ignored.
Put your Beliefs about A in Descriptive Terms:

____

____

____

____

Consequences (Actions): How have you behaved when you enounter issues with your partner?
Example: When my partner insists on talking I get annoyed. If my partner pushes the point I shut down and I even get angry sometimes.
Put your Actions in Descriptive Terms:

____

____

____

____

Re Direction

Re Direction

Q X T C J F B E W L W P B O G U V

W R T F O R M A L O U C B X H Z Y

R H H Q K N V U G C V F F L C R X

O G O V S I D K B B F Q A E A R D

C D U L J D M I Y W Y I X T F O O

R B G B I B V S T L C K I V K G P

K P H L S S P P B I F L E N N F N

Y D T B M F T G F B O A B I I X X

Z P W Y R F X I U S R N H D D G O

U V D P K G T W C V M C I K H J P

S L D M P R A O W F A X U N W K V

C X F V A C D R E O T R N K G B B

J Z X T B I X K C K T E S T Q D I

S L M R R P F B G Q I G U Y Y W Z

Z Y F B O F D O R A N G U T A N K

C Z K B Z T V O L D G J S T W U H

G O G A W E R K U Q H S M F W K Z

FORMAL
WORKBOOK
ORANGUTAN
CONDITIONING

THOUGHT
HOLISTIC
ARTIFICIAL

SOLITARY
COACHING
FORMATTING

Has sadness been a struggle for you lately?
What do you feel contributes to why you are sad?

____

____

____

Belief vs Behavior

Activating Event: "I feel very sad"
Put the Activating Event in your own words:

____

Belief: I will never be happy?
Example: I put everything into my career. I do not
feel as though I can ever have success like that again.
Put your Beliefs in Descriptive Terms:

____

____

____

____

Consequences (Actions): You resist opportunities to
start something new citing your lack of interest.
Instead it feels better to just stay in bed.
Example: You loose your job. You feel sad and like
things will not get better? So, you ___________.
(Unhealthy vs Healthy Coping)
Put your Action Response in Descriptive Terms:

____

____

____

____

Re DiRection

1	2	3	4	5	6	7	8	9	10	11	12	13	14	15	16
		12		16			13	14							
		7	8						3	1		6	2		13
	5						7						3		
4				15	5	14	8	2		7					
	14		6		16	1				10			13		7
9	13	4	12					3					15	16	
	16					12	15							11	4
	11		1				14					8		2	6
1				11			12		16	5	2			7	14
	8	14	11	1				7				13	4		2
6	12				7	10			14					3	
		16	10		14	4			11					9	1
		5	12		11	10		15		4	14		1	13	
	1	11							7	2			10		
	2			15					1		11		12		5
		14					1	9	6	12		11			

Find something happy to listen to online!

B C J J W G G X R Q Y Y M W J X
U A O X W G V U U G R Q M V W J
S L Y M G X T T B Y H O T I J Z
I M F B P J A N X M V A Y M E Q
N H U K H L W J E L C V Q U T P
E A L C Y K I K C R L Y F K A W
S P N F C O N C E S S I O N U I
S P E O Q C N C A J Z L L F N W
N I S O Y W E A T T G F X N L F
X E S G G J R U H P E W O U S N
H S B Z J F H Q I C N D F F B C
N T B C Z P J O Z D D E L E T E
B W T Z D U N O A A C L I L B O
J P S C O L V L Q A M E A G I N
U P C R X A S Z E S P R S I J V
Q J H Y H A P P Y A Z Y B U Y W

CALM
WINNER
HAPPIEST
COMPLICATED

HAPPY
BUSINESS
JOYFULNESS

DELETE
PEACEFUL
CONCESSION

Name a life situation that usually makes you panic? Ex. Relocating

____

____

Belief vs Behavior

Activating Event: "My child is failing in college."
Put the Activating Event in your own words:

____

Belief: What are you thinking about when you encounter an overwhelming situation?
Example: If my child fails out of college it will be a waste of money and an embarrassment!
Put your Beliefs in Descriptive Terms:

____

____

____

____

Consequences (Actions): How do you react when you encounter an overwhelming situation?
Example: When you are unable to fix an issue do you lash out, shut down or put work on overdrive?
Put your Actions in Descriptive Terms:

____

____

____

What did you want to be when you grew up? What did you become?

Belief vs Behavior

Activating Event: Name something dissatisfying about work.

Put the Activating Event in your own words:

____

Belief: What do you expect out of a job?

Example: If I get a good job then I will have good co-workers, feel useful, and live a financially sound life.

Put your Beliefs about work in Descriptive Terms:

____

____

____

Consequences (Actions): How do you behave when things do not go as expected at work?

Example: I hate this job. Every morning is like a jail sentence but I can't seem to find a better job right now.

Put your Actions in Descriptive Terms:

____

____

____

Re Direction

Does Your Smile
Portray How You
Really Feel Inside?

Belief vs Behavior

Activating Event: Describe a time when you had to wear a social mask.
Put the Activating Event in your own words:

____

Belief: How do you see social situations?

Example: I will never fit in socially I would rather stay indoors. Going out leads to drama.
Put your Beliefs in Descriptive Terms:

____

____

____

____

Consequences (Actions): How do you behave when you have to be in social settings?

Example: The networking party is mandatory. You hate the idea of going. How do you respond?
Put your Actions in Descriptive Terms:

____

____

____

Re Direction

Unscramble the words below.
Answer key is on page 23

UMEENSATM	=	AROYLITS	=
UHTGOTH	=	SSBIL	=
HERCE	=	ENCNTTENMTO	=
NLIAETO	=	LGTDIEH	=
ILCISOTH	=	AOINHCGC	=
IPUREAOH	=	LCAM	=
ACLEFUPE	=	PYHPA	=
METEXTNEIC	=	LYUFOJ	=
HRIMT	=	PESAURLE	=
ELDITPCAMOC	=	CGRJONIIE	=
OTSAAITFCSIN	=	EYTREINS	=
OTNVIACA	=	IFLEER	=
RTILUNAITQY	=	LRIDSBEEA	=
LZEA	=	SEICUR	=
CCUSSSE	=	AFBEASKTR	=
CHUNRB	=	DRMEINTENI	=
OYJ	=	DAGL	=
IERLNHXATOIA	=	JBULEEI	=
EYJMENTNO	=	SAYSTCE	=
IEGAYT	=	RREYM	=

What are you good at that you also enjoy doing?

____

____

____

____

Belief vs Behavior

Activating Event (Thought): "My career is not satisfying,"
Put the Activating Thought in your own words:

____

Belief: I am not operating in my passion? If I could monetize my passion then I could be happy with work.
Example:
Put your Beliefs in Descriptive Terms:

____

____

____

Consequences (Actions): How is your inability to live out your passion expressed in your behavior?
Example: I always wonder what may have been and it makes me hate where I am in life?
Put your Actions in Descriptive Terms:

____

____

____

Re Direction Word Scramble - Unscramble (Answers in Red)

UMEENSATM	AMUSEMENT
UHTGOTH	THOUGHT
HERCE	CHEER
NLIAETO	ELATION
ILCISOTH	HOLISTIC
IPUREAOH	EUPHORIA
ACLEFUPE	PEACEFUL
METEXTNEIC	EXCITEMENT
HRIMT	MIRTH
ELDITPCAMOC	COMPLICATED
OTSAAITFCSIN	SATISFACTION
OTNVIACA	VACATION
RTILUNAITQY	TRANQUILITY
LZEA	ZEAL
CCUSSSE	SUCCESS
CHUNRB	BRUNCH
OYJ	JOY
IERLNHXATOIA	EXHILARATION
EYJMENTNO	ENJOYMENT
IEGAYT	GAIETY
AROYLITS	SOLITARY
SSBIL	BLISS
ENCNTTENMTO	CONTENTMENT
LGTDIEH	DELIGHT
AOINHCGC	COACHING
LCAM	CALM
PYHPA	HAPPY
LYUFOJ	JOYFUL
PESAURLE	PLEASURE
CGRJONIIE	REJOICING
EYTREINS	SERENITY
IFLEER	RELIEF
LRIDSBEEA	DESIRABLE
SEICUR	CRUISE
AFBEASKTR	BREAKFAST
DRMEINTENI	DINNERTIME
DAGL	GLAD
JBULEEI	JUBILEE
SAYSTCE	ECSTASY
RREYM	MERRY

coping

What makes you uniquely you?

Belief vs Behavior

Activating Event: "I do not like social events"
Put the Activating Event in your own words:

____

Belief: I'm weird, people do not get me and I do not get them.
Example: As soon as I walked in they stared at me. I know they are judging me. I am so uncomfortable.
Put your Beliefs in Descriptive Terms:

____

____

____

____

Consequences (Actions) These people get me. I do not care that they use drugs sometimes.
Example: Choosing to hang out with nice people who are doing unhealthy things in order to avoid lonliness.
Put your Actions in Descriptive Terms:

____

____

____

____

In what way has trauma limited you?

____

Belief vs Behavior

Activating Event: This traumatic event makes me damaged goods.
Put the Activating Event in your own words:

____

Belief: Because I went through that I will never be a whole person or have a happy life.
Example: That hurt me so bad that I cannot move on. All I can do is think about what hurt me.
Put your Beliefs in Descriptive Terms:

____

____

____

____

Consequences (Actions) No can ever love the real me. If anyone ever knew my secret they would think Im damaged goods too.
Example: No one can ever know this secret. I can never forget and I will never move on.
Put your Actions in Descriptive Terms:

____

____

____

Has the quest for success impacted how you feel about yourself?

Belief vs Behavior

Activating Event: "Trying to achieve my goals is becoming harder and harder"
Put the Activating Event in your own words:

____

Belief: If I am not able to achieve my goals then what good am I to my family or myself?
Example: I am a failure and every time I am passed over for the raise it confirms that.
Put your Beliefs in Descriptive Terms:

____

____

____

____

Consequences (Actions): If I have failed so much already then it is impossible for me to find success.
Example: I was told I need a degree for the raise and I could barely get out of high school. I could never get a degree.
Put your Actions in Descriptive Terms:

____

____

____

____

Has disappointment impacted how you see your present and future?

Belief vs Behavior

Activating Event: "Another disappointing outcome"
Put the Activating Event in your own words:

____

Belief: I try and try but I know I will never make it.
Example: Everything I try seems like it is working and then something happens, What is the point anymore.
Put your Beliefs in Descriptive Terms:

____

____

____

____

Consequences (Actions) Instead of trying to do something big I will just stay in my lane.
Example: This is making me so angry. I just rather not even try to get ahead anymore.
Put your Actions in Descriptive Terms:

____

____

____

____

Is it easy for you to address your health?

____

Belief vs Behavior

Activating Event: "I have been coughing for a while"
Put the Activating Event in your own words:

____

Belief: I am at the same age that my dad started having health problems. I will probably have similar issues.
Example: I cannot believe I am old enough to need a prostate check. This is not going to go well.
Put your Beliefs in Descriptive Terms:

____

____

____

____

Consequences (Actions): How do you behave when you have to go to the doctor?
Example: I am sick to my stomach but I keep hesitating to make the appointment because I'm scared of the results.
Put your Actions in Descriptive Terms:

____

____

____

____

What are some situations that make you feel powerless?

Belief vs Behavior

Activating Event: "Something that makes you feel poweless."
Put the Activating Event in your own words:

____

Belief: If I cannot fix the situation then I am powerless.
Example: My brother is dying and I'm letting him down. I should be able to do something more than visit!
Put your Beliefs in Descriptive Terms:

____

____

____

____

Consequences (Actions): How do you behave when you encounter a situation that you cannot change?
Example: I know my brother wants to see me but, I cannot bear to see him in the hospital. Im meeting my friends at the bar instead.
Put your Actions in Descriptive Terms:

____

____

____

____

Are the things you fear talking about causing you to feel bound?

Belief vs Behavior

Activating Event: "I have a life changing secret"
Put the Activating Event in your own words:

____

Belief: What do you believe this secret means about who you are and how will it impact you if it is found out?
Example: Everyone will think it is my fault and I will be seen as dirty, just for nothing to be fixed.
Put your Beliefs in Descriptive Terms:

____

____

____

____

Consequences (Actions): How do you react to the experience you detailed in A?
Example: When your emotionally hurt do you want to lash out in anger, keep it in or vent?
Put your Actions in Descriptive Terms:

____

____

____

____

What did you expect your family life to be like when you became an adult?

____

Belief vs Behavior

Activating Event: "Not having help has made my family life very stressful"
Put the Activating Event in your own words:

____

Belief: What is your family life supposed to look like?
Example: My husband and my kids are supposed to be the happiest factors in my life.
Put your Beliefs in Descriptive Terms:

____

____

____

____

Consequences (Actions): How does stress impact your interactions with your spouse and kids?
Example: My kids are driving me crazy and my spouse is not emotionally available. I'm short and annoyed. I just want everyone to leave me alone.
Put your Actions in Descriptive Terms:

____

____

____

____

Belief vs Behavior

Activating Event: "Dealing with the effect of how my problem is affecting others"

Put the Activating Event in your own words:

____

Belief: Kids have to do what their parents say.

Example: When I was growing up my parents did not ask me how I felt when they made decisions.

Put your Beliefs in Descriptive Terms:

____

____

____

____

Consequences (Actions): Things are spinning out of control with the kids ever since my spouse and I split up?

Example: The kids' behavior has changed. I cannot calm them down. They have even become disrespectful. I am considering going to therapy.

Put your Actions in Descriptive Terms:

____

____

____

Belief vs Behavior

Activating Event: "Dealling with a break-up."
Put the Activating Event in your own words:

____

Belief: This break-up hurts so bad. If she doesn't
want me then nobody ever will.
Example: This was the most connected to a person I
have ever felt. If this is over I will never find love.
Put your Beliefs in Descriptive Terms:

____

____

____

____

Consequences (Actions): How do you react to issues
arising in your relationship?
Example: Do you stay sad? Do you become
vindictive? Or do you move on quickly?
Put your Actions in Descriptive Terms:

____

____

____

____

Belief vs Behavior

Activating Event: "A relationship problem."
Put the Activating Event in your own words:

____

Belief: If we have to go to therapy then it just is not worth the trouble?
Example: I am not the problem. She may need therapy but, I do not!
Put your Beliefs in Descriptive Terms:

____

____

____

____

Consequences (Actions): I keep meeting people who are not right for me.
Example: We never see eye to eye? I do not understand why I always end up with people like this.
Put your Actions in Descriptive Terms:

____

____

____

____

Do you believe in a higher power?

Belief vs Behavior

Activating Event: "I have issues with spirituality"
Put the Activating Event in your own words:

____

Belief: What is your perspective on religion?
Example: My mom always went to church, but I do not see where it did anything for her.
Put your Beliefs in Descriptive Terms:

____

____

____

____

Consequences (Actions): I am not sure how I feel about a higher power?
Example: I do not like how my mom always put the church before the kids. I don't want to know her God.
Put your Actions in Descriptive Terms:

____

____

____

____

I LOVE MYSELF

Belief vs Behavior

Activating Event: "I need to forgive myself"
Put the Activating Event in your own words:

____

Belief: I make bad decisions for myself and always put myself last?
Example: I really want to relax today but my sister wants a ride to the mall. I guess I have to go to the mall.
Put your Beliefs in Descriptive Terms:

____

____

____

____

Consequences (Actions): I am angry and taking it out on myself because I should have said no.
Example: I did not plan to spend the day at the mall. Now I am extra tired, sad and angry at myself because I did not get a chance to rest.
Put your Actions in Descriptive Terms:

____

____

____

I am...

What are 3 things you plan to implement when you are struggling to feel emotionally well?

Belief vs Behavior

Activating Event: "I am bored"
Put the Activating Event in your own words:

____

Belief: What are your beliefs about engaging in activities?
Example: It is too hard and it costs too much for me to get around since my accident. Everything is a painful journey.
Put your Beliefs in Descriptive Terms:

____

____

____

____

Consequences (Actions): How does your belief in B affect your actions?
Example: There is a group for accident survivors and they do activities, but I already know its going to be hard and a big headache.
Put your Actions in Descriptive Terms:

____

____

____

When were you the happiest?

____

Re Direction

Find Your Relaxation

Re Direction

4					10		5	11		14	9		13		16
15			16					8	7			2		5	
11		14			13		12	3		10	5	9	15		
	8	5	12		7						16	11	4		
			4			12				11		5	3		10
		7			5	1			16						
	5		13	11		2	16	9			10				
12			2	10		6		14	13				9	16	1
5				2	15			7		13			8	4	
2					14	11	6	16			1				7
	7	12	3		1					15		13			2
		4	1					5	11	2				3	15
	12				16	8		2	3						
		1	9	6				4	5						8
	15			3	11		10	1	14	8		4			
14				12	5			13			6				

Find Your Coping Mechanisms

Re Direction

C1	C2	C3	C4	C5	C6	C7	C8	C9	C10	C11	C12	C13	C14	C15	C16
							6	9					8		
						3		14			16	5	10	9	12
			10	2				12			4				
				9					8			3		4	14
10		14	1	12				16		4			6		9
					2	14					13			10	
7		2		3	13	16		11			10		1	12	8
					4								14	3	
8					3		10	4			7				2
	15	10							1					5	
11						13	12					14	4		
			7		6	8				3		11			
	10	11	5		8			2				12			
						1		4				10			13
	13					2	7	10			14	6		8	4
			8		6					2			14		

coping

Mood Tracker

J F M A M J J A S O N D

1
2
3
4
5
6
7
8
9
10
11
12
13
14
15
16
17
18
19
20
21
22
23
24
25
26
27
28
29
30
31

- AMAZING
- HAPPY
- NORMAL
- EXCITED
- STRESSED
- FOCUSED
- TIRED / EXHAUSTED
- DEPRESSED / SAD
- SICK
- LOW ENERGY
- NERVOUS / ANXIOUS
- ANGRY

Assign color to a specific mood and color the squares according to your mood

Date:

Quote Of The Day

Today I am truly grateful for...

Here's what would make today great...

I am...

Some amazing things that happened today...

Some amazing things that happened today...

What could I have done to make today even better?

Re Direction

Re Direction

		11	1				8		7						
	6						7	16		9					
	8			11				6					16		
						9		2					7		
					6		14	3				10	2		
		7	15								12			16	
1					16								8		
							5				15	3			
				12		15		13			11			2	
13			8		7		2	10			5				11
						8				6		14		5	
			2			1		4	12	15	8			7	
8			9								16				
					15			5	13	10		1			
7	16			5						12					
	10			1				15	2	7	6				

W U T F K X R Y R X O L J C D M

V F F Q C P Z X O N Z N O F R C

M J R U T R C T A S C C M C M V

J D C T Q O U R C T P P B Q G Y

E M E N H M R I G Y B P J R G L

N C K S N O T T S Z X E P V E W

O U M L T T A D I E L E O V X D

M L O Y C I I U G F W F A V B E

F A J D X O N K H F J R H J O S

I X W N F N V A C A T I O N I I

B R E A K F A S T M Y M S V W R

F I L T E R U X E I R K A S C A

G B W T B F E L Y H O S Q M I B

V A B U S R Q B L P Z N Q T P L

H X K C I L M M U L B E A C H E

T W O S R C X D O E S U F C L D

BEACH	FILTER	TRAVEL
CRUISE	CURTAIN	VACATION
PROMOTION	DESIRABLE	BREAKFAST
DESTINATION		

ReDirection

Open YOUr Mind

Therapeutic Maze and Activity Coloring Book

@2023
Www.HolisticCoaching.info
~ Google: Holistic Coaching, St Pete

Find Us On Social Media:
Facebook and LinkedIn: Jan Harp & Holistic Coaching
YouTube: HolisticBiz Coaching

Contact the Author Regarding all Duplication Requests and
for Bulk Order Pricing
For Business Development Services Visit:
Www.HolisticBizMarketing.com